# In the Beginning
### Genesis 1

Written and Produced by Gwen Shamblin
Illustrated by Erin Shamblin

Copyright © 2010
by Gwen Shamblin and Erin Shamblin

All rights reserved.

No part of this publication may be stored in a retrieval system, transmitted, or reproduced in any way, including but not limited to photocopy, photograph, magnetic or other record, without prior arrangement and written permission of the publisher.

Printed in the United States.
Weigh Down Ministries and Remnant Publishing

Weigh Down Ministries
P.O. Box 689099, Franklin, TN 37068-9099
www.weighdown.com
1-800-844-5208

ISBN 1-892729-11-3

The sale of the voluminous literature from Weigh Down Ministries is not for a profit. The money is used for the print and duplication of materials and any additional money is returned to God's Church to reprint or reproduce or produce any other materials. The revelations and the word of God is not for sale but freely given to those who cannot afford to pay for the reprinting of these words and videos and audios that are used solely for the furthering of the Kingdom of the One and Only God of the Universe. May they be used to make His True Nature known so that all will lovingly bow down to Him and adoringly praise Him forever and ever. Amen.

This book is dedicated to all of God's children—those that are lost and those that have found their way home.

In the very, very beginning of time, God created the heavens and the earth.

At first it was empty and dark, but God said, "Let there be light" and he called the light "day." The darkness he called "night" and so there was evening and morning—the very first day! And God saw the light was good.

For the parents: What would it be like if everything was dark? Praise God for the light!

On the second (2) day, God separated the waters above the earth from the waters below. He called this space "sky."

Introduce the concept of evaporation, which is one way God continues to separate the water on earth from the water in the sky.

On the third (3) day, God made the dry ground appear. God called it "land" and he gathered the waters and he called it "seas." God saw that it was good. Then God said, "Let the land produce plants and trees."

Find the trees and plants in the picture and explain that God made thousands of different trees and plants, all with different leaves. Talk about the beach and the sand, and even if you've never been, describe to them how beautiful it is.

On the fourth (4) day, God made the sun and the moon and the stars in the sky. God saw that it was good.

Ask the children to point to the earth, the sun, and the moon, and to find all the stars. Ask them if they like night lights; God made night lights for the entire earth. It is so beautiful!

**O**n the fifth (5) day, God created all the different fish in the ocean… and he blessed them so that their number would increase in the ocean. In other words, so that they could have baby fish till the sea was full of them.

And he created all the different birds in the sky… and he blessed them so that they could have baby birds so that their number would increase till the birds would fill the earth.

Help the children find the whales, dolphins, fish, turtle, octopus, stingray, seagulls and birds.

On the sixth (6) day, God created all the different animals in the world... and all the livestock for the farms. Then God said, "Let us make man in our image, in our likeness..." So God created male and female [man and woman] in his own image and let them rule over the birds of the air, over the livestock, over all the earth, and over all the creatures. So God created man and woman in his own image. Their names were Adam and Eve. God blessed them so that they could have babies and increase in number. God gave man food and he let them eat plants and the fruit from the trees, and he gave every creature that had breath in it as food to eat. God saw that it was VERY good.

Help the children find the man, lion, elephant, giraffe, sheep, bird, rabbit, and lizard. Since man was made in God's image, it gives us a picture of what God looks like.

By the seventh (7) day, God had finished all the work he had been doing and so he rested from all his work. And God blessed the seventh day and made it holy because he rested.

God worked hard for six days and rested on the seventh day. So God has asked us to work for six days and rest on the seventh day. What he wants us to do is think about all he has done and praise him and sing to him on that day, called the Sabbath.

"There are six days when you may work, but the seventh day is a Sabbath of rest, a day of sacred assembly. You are not to do any work; wherever you live, it is a Sabbath to the LORD." Lev. 23:3

Gwen, the founder of Weigh Down Ministries and a founding member of the Remnant Fellowship Churches, is the happy "GiGi" of five grandchildren! She loves God and she loves God's children big and small—old and young. Her defining characteristic is her deep love for the Heavenly Father, which she found by following in the footsteps of Jesus Christ.

Gwen believes that: "The world would be a better place if we all just listen to Jesus who said to focus on the Father, His will, and finishing His work on earth. May His Kingdom come and His will be done—just as it is in Heaven. Nothing makes you more full of love for God and others. The way to raise your children is to love God." Her prayer is that people everywhere find this love and connection with the Most High God by putting Him first in all that they do. She has been married for many years to her husband, David, and has two married children—Michael, who is married to Erin, and Elizabeth, who is married to Brandon Hannah.

GWEN WITH HER GRANDCHILDREN: GRACIE, GWENETH, GARLAND, GABRIELE, & GLORIA.

Gwen's Prayer: "We come before You praying for the children of Zion. We pray that they are strong and focused on You and Your will. We pray that they learn to love You through obedience. We pray that they learn to walk in the paths that Jesus walked in—loving You first and doing exactly what You wanted Him to do. May Your children always seek Your Kingdom and Your righteousness first for then we know that everything else will be added unto them. In Jesus' Name, Amen."

# Give your children what they need to grow up in love with God.

The Zion Kids series was developed and produced by Gwen Shamblin, founder of Weigh Down Ministries and best-selling author of *Weigh Down Diet*. A mother of two grown children and grandmother to five beautiful girls, Gwen saw a need in the current children's video market for lessons that combined fundamental educational principles with precious instruction about God and His Word.

The Zion Kids series of DVD lessons will bring joy and fun to the entire family! Each activity-packed 30-minute lesson will combine fundamental preschool and elementary instruction alongside age-appropriate Bible stories, moral lessons, and music that will get feet of all ages jumping and dancing in praise to the Father! Children will learn about God's beautiful creation through nature, animals, music, friendships, and more! Fun-filled settings and lessons will guide children through their ABCs, counting, colors, and shapes. And best of all, every lesson in Zion Kids will point viewers of all ages directly back up to God and Christ in praise and prayer—because, like it says in Zion Kids, "It's all about GOD!"

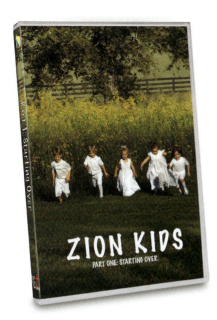

Zion Kids Part One:
Starting Over

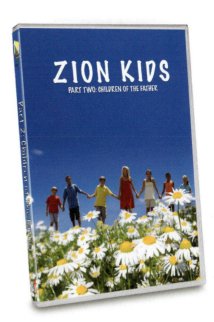

Zion Kids Part Two:
Children of the Father

Zion Kids Part Three:
Doing the Will of God

Zion Kids Part Four:
All Things Point Up to God

# Zion Kids Book: *A to Zion*

A to Zion is an Inspirational Alphabet Book that will teach your child from a very young age how everything is about God!!! This book is for all ages and will point the whole family up to God as you enjoy reading together.

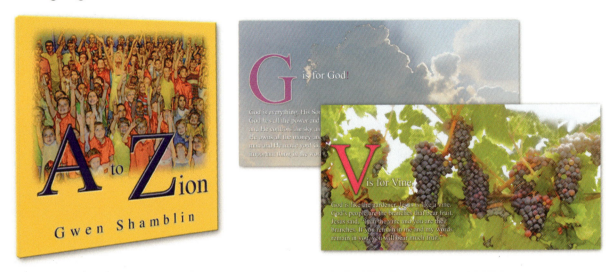

The letters and pictures will create lots of fun conversation which will bring you and your children closer together.

## Coming Soon!

*Children's Bible Lessons*: Sign up on our mailing list to be notified about this exciting project! www.WeighDown.com

# Resources for the Parents:

- *Feeding Children Physically and Spiritually Series*: Practical advice ranging from nutrition to help with overeating to spiritual needs.
- *The Last Exodus*: A great class to do as a family. Basic weight loss seminar for ages 8-28. This seminar is geared towards teenagers and young adults, and is positively affecting all ages! If you have ever felt yourself entrapped or addicted to anything in this world, this is the program for you! Go to WeighDown.com to watch a free orientation.
- *Zion Kids: Lessons for the Parents:* a moving collection of 2 DVD lessons from Gwen Shamblin that are centered on raising children to wholeheartedly love and obey the Father!
- *Audio CDs/MP3:* "Motherhood: Pregnancy & Infancy" and "Raising Godly Children."
- Visit us regularly at *WeighDown.com* for the latest parenting resources that will help your children and your family love God more every day. Click on "Store/Library" and look for the "Parenting" and "Children's Products (under age 15)" categories for these resources and more.
- *Truthstream:* become a member of our monthly subscriber program where you get access via the Internet to hundreds of Weigh Down Audios and Videos and music including talks on weight loss, parenting, marriage, anger, depression and more!
- *Weigh Down Web Radio*: WDWB airs Weigh Down messages, testimonies, music, and media clips surrounding its life-changing impact on people's lives. We're "on the air" 24 hours a day, 7 days a week, 365 days a year!

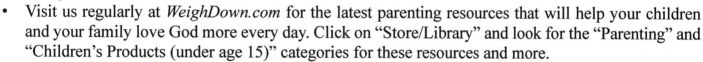

# Other Titles and Seminars by This Author:

- *Weigh Down Basics Seminar*: 6-week audio and video series for adults to help you lose any excess weight.
- *Weigh Down Diet* book (over 1 million sold): Basic weight loss instruction to help you lose your excess pregnancy weight.
- *Rise Above* book: Follow-up book to *Weigh Down Diet*, when you are ready for more.
- *Exodus Out of Egypt: The CHANGE Series*: The next step in your weight loss, eight-week seminar.

For more information about Zion Kids, or Weigh Down Ministries,
please call us at 1-800-844-5208, or visit the following websites:

www.WeighDown.com     www.GwenShamblin.com     www.RemnantFellowship.org

CPSIA information can be obtained at www.ICGtesting.com
Printed in the USA
LVIW01n0809040517
533088LV00001B/1